Our Land
and
Heritage

Our Neighborhoods

by Eleanor Thomas

with Ernest W. Tiegs and Fay Adams

Ginn and Company

Contents

© Copyright, 1979,
by Ginn and Company (Xerox Corporation)
All Rights Reserved
Home Office: Lexington, Massachusetts 02173
0-663-36143-5

3 We need clothes

4 We need to communicate

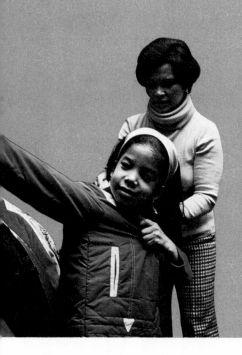

5 We travel in many ways

6 Getting to know Japan

Maps

We need neighbors

A new place to live

Steve and Penny have moved.
They have moved to Eastfield.
They have no friends here.

How does it feel to have
no friends?

A new friend

Anne has come to see
Penny and Steve.
She lives next door.
She is their neighbor.
She will be a friend.

A new home

Steve and Penny have a new home.
It is in Eastfield.
Their home is an old house.
The family likes an old house.
Why do you think they do?

Mother and Father like to fix things.
The old house has many things to fix.
That is why they like the old house.

Steve and Penny like the big yard.
Can you guess why?

Mother and Steve are working.
Father and Penny are working, too.
They are fixing a window in the attic.
Where is the attic?

"Here is an old oil lamp," said Father.
"It helped light this house long ago.
Oil was a good fuel for lights.

"People still use oil.
We will use oil
to heat this house."

Oil is important

Refineries make gasoline from oil.
Cars are run with gasoline.
Trains are run with oil.
Refineries make jet airplane fuel from oil.

People use more and more oil.
We should be careful how we use it.
We may use up all of the oil
in the world.
Then what will we do?

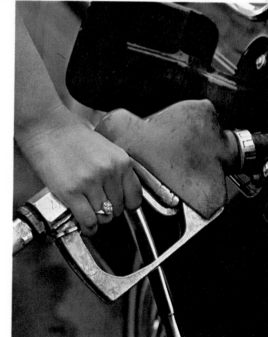

What can we do to save oil?
How can you help?

How can we use
the wind to help us?

How can we use
the sun
to help us?

Many kinds of fuel

There are many kinds of fuel.

Wood is a fuel.
Wood comes from trees.

Coal is a fuel, too.
Coal comes from under
the ground.

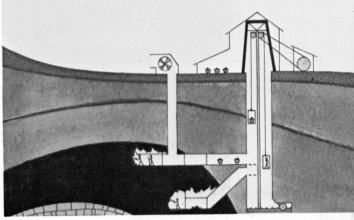

Oil also comes
from under the ground.
Oil is the fuel we use most.

Are there some other fuels?

A trip to long ago

Penny and Steve gave the oil lamp
to the museum.
Miss Park at the museum thanked them.
"We have just the place for the lamp,"
she said.

Penny and Steve saw pictures
of long ago at the museum.

This is a picture of the place
where Eastfield now is.

What does this picture in the museum show?
It shows the river.
It shows the village of the Mohegan people.

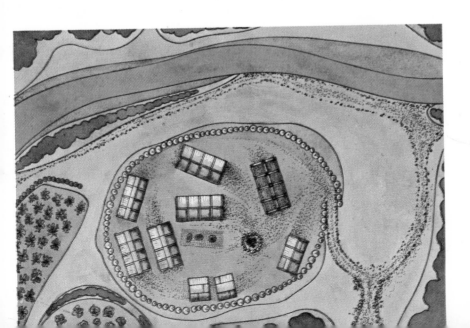

The map
is of the same place.
Find the river
on the map.
Find the Mohegan
village.

Many settlers came to the river.
They cut down trees to build houses.
They cut down trees to make fields.
They built fences around the fields.

At first there were no stores in Eastfield.
The settlers had to make many things.
They had to grow their own food.

Many settlers grew wheat.
One settler had a mill
to grind wheat into flour.

How could the settlers
help one another?

Later a railroad was built.
Trains stopped at Eastfield.
The railroad helped Eastfield grow.

"This is the way Eastfield
looked then," said Miss Park.
"See the center of Eastfield."

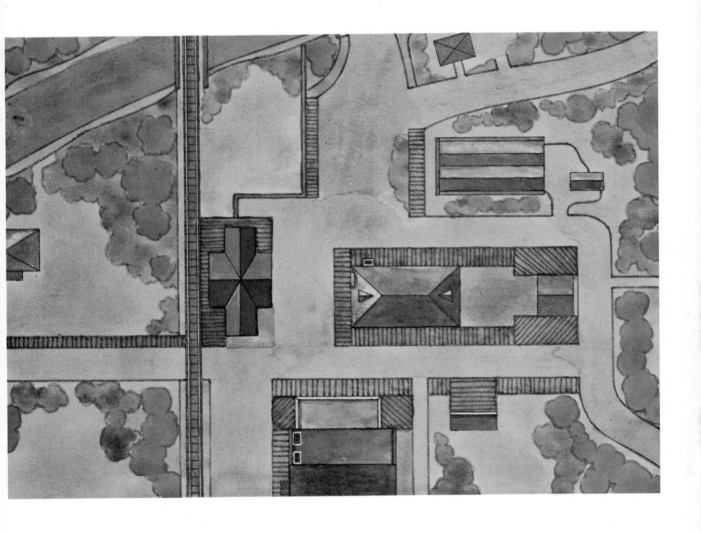

This is a map of the center of Eastfield.
Find the railroad.
Find the hotel.

Exploring Eastfield

Anne took Penny and Steve exploring.
First they saw the park.
It was beautiful.

Long ago a woman came to Eastfield
from Italy.
She came to Eastfield to live.
Later she gave her land to Eastfield.
The land was used for the park.
People worked to make
the park beautiful.

20

Next they saw
the fire station.
How do workers
at the fire station help us?

Then the children went to the library.
How do workers at the library help us?

Anne said, "Let's go down town.
We can look in the windows of the stores."

"Now we are in the center
of Eastfield," said Anne.
"My father works here.
He works in this bank."

"Mother and Father use this bank,"
said Steve.
"They put money in it.
They use money to buy food and clothes.
They use money to buy fuel.
They used money to buy our house."

The children walked along.

They saw the big store on the corner.
"I have been in that store," Penny said.
"Mother bought my winter coat there."

Next they met a police officer
and a little boy.
The little boy was lost.
The officer will help him.
She will find the boy's home.

How does it feel to be lost?

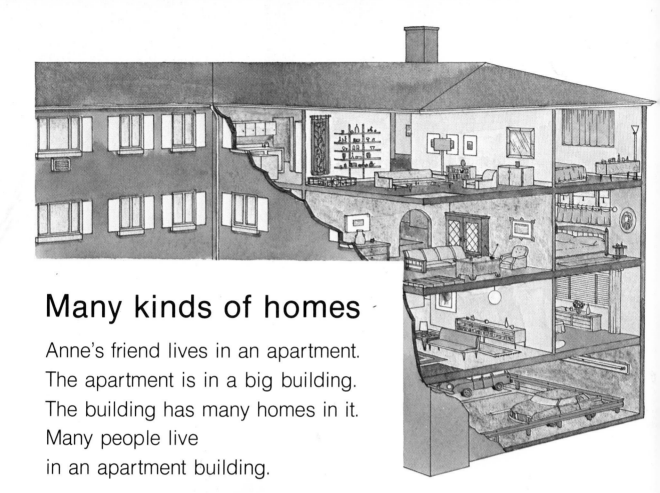

Many kinds of homes

Anne's friend lives in an apartment.
The apartment is in a big building.
The building has many homes in it.
Many people live
in an apartment building.

Homes are where people live.
There are many kinds of homes.

A map helps you find your way

The map shows the center of Eastfield.
It shows where Steve and Penny live, too.

The map key helps you read the map.
Use the map key to find Steve's and Penny's home.
Find their home on the map.

Find the bank on the map key.
Find the bank on the map.
Find the fire station.
Find the park.

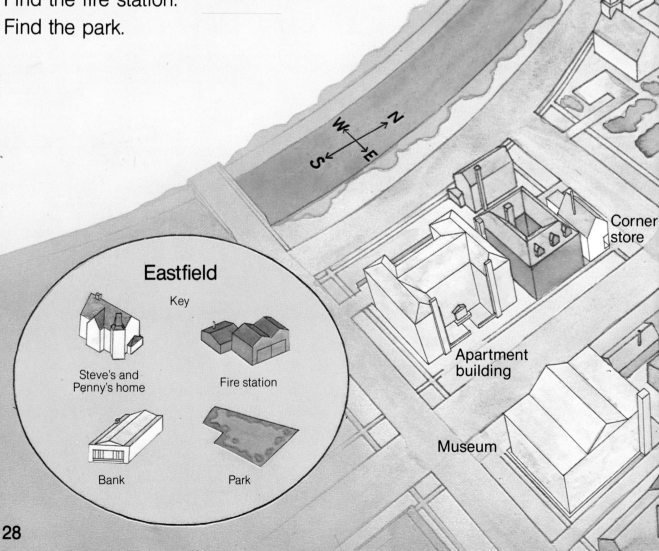

Corner store

Apartment building

Museum

Eastfield

Key

Steve's and Penny's home

Fire station

Bank

Park

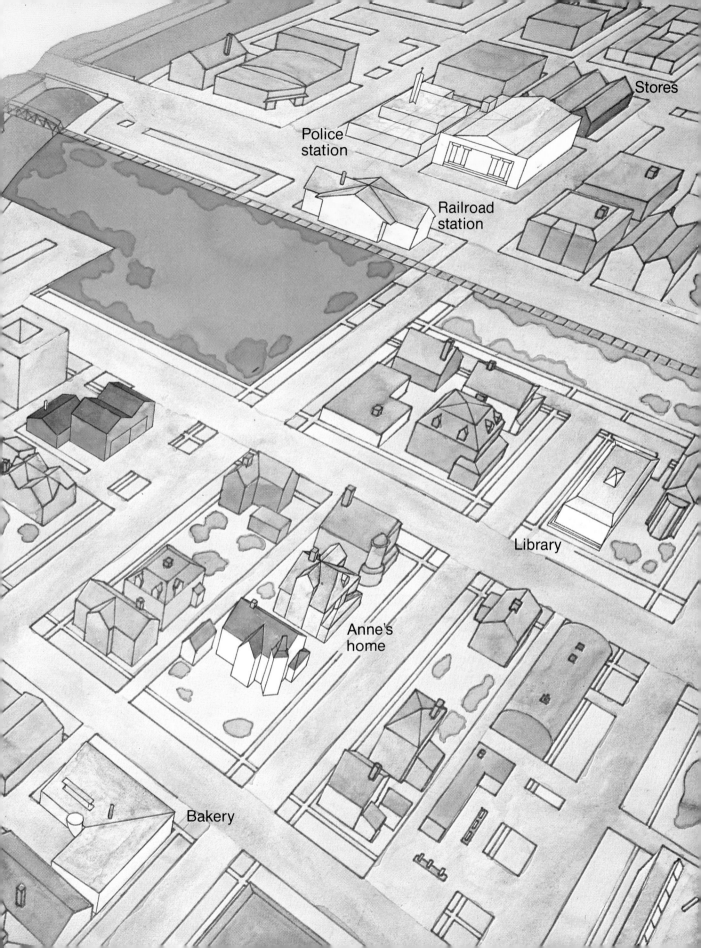

Stores

Police
station

Railroad
station

Library

Anne's
home

Bakery

The seasons in Eastfield

Penny and Steve and Anne
explored Eastfield in the fall.
In fall people get ready for winter.
How do they get ready?

There will be snow
in the winter.

Plants start to grow in the spring.
People plant gardens in the spring.
Sunshine and rain help plants grow.

Summer in Eastfield is warm.
Plants grow in the warm summer.

Winter in different places

Winter in Eastfield is cold.
It snows in the winter in Eastfield.
Do you have snow in winter
where you live?

Winter is not the same
in all places.
What is winter like in Hawaii?
What is winter like in Japan?
What is winter like in Florida?

2
We need food

To the Littles' orchard

"I am going to the Littles' orchard,"
said Mr. Hunt.
"Who wants to go with me?"

"I do," said Chris.

"So do I," said Janet.

"Wait for me," said Bill.
"I like to pick apples."

"You can see the orchard from this hill,"
said Mr. Hunt.
"We can pick fresh apples now.
We can put them in our big basket.
We may fill a basket for two dollars."

"We pay less for apples
if we pick them," said Janet.
"We would have to pay much more
at the store."

"I see three workers with you,"
said Mrs. Little.
"Each worker must have a basket.
Pick all the apples you want.
Then we'll go to the house.
I have a surprise for you."

"We will be careful,"
said Mr. Hunt.
"We will not break any branches."

Mr. Little is also working in the orchard.

"We have workers to help us," he said.
"Some workers pick apples.
Others pack the apples into boxes.
Still other workers put the boxes on trucks.
We pay them all for their work."

"It would be fun to work
in an orchard," said Janet.

The children went to the house
for the surprise.

"Mrs. Little has made apple butter
and baked bread," said Bill.
"It smells so good in here."

A big pumpkin was on the table.
It was to be a Halloween pumpkin.

What will the Littles do
with the pumpkins left in the field?

Where jams and jellies are made

Jams and jellies are made
in a large factory.
Trucks bring the apples
from large orchards.
Other fruit also comes here
in trucks.
Some fruit comes by fast trains
and jets from places far away.

Berries come from farms nearby.
They also come from other places.
They are picked and cleaned.
Only the best berries are used.

Some berries are quick frozen
at the factory.
Berries do not spoil
while they are frozen.
They keep their good flavor.
They are used later to make
jam and jelly.

They are cooked quickly
at the factory.
They are made into jams
and jellies.

The jams and jellies
are put into clean jars.
The jars go from machine
to machine.

Workers test the fruit used in the factory.
They test the jams and jellies, too.
They test to see if the flavor is good.
They work to find the best way
to make jams and jellies.

Trucks take the jams and jellies
to food stores.

The dairy farm

Eastfield has many dairy farms around it.
There are many cows on a dairy farm.
The cows give milk.
People on the farms prepare the milk
for people in the city.

There is much work to do every day.
The cows must have food and water.
They must be kept clean.
They must be milked
 two times a day.

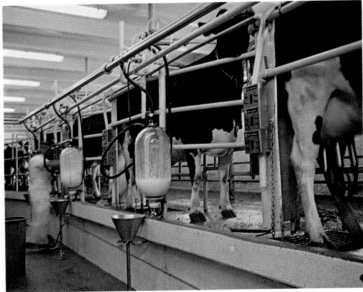

Machines are used to milk the cows.
The machines must be kept clean.
The barns must be kept clean.
This work must be done every day.

Dairy farmers must plan the work well.

The cows must be healthy.
Special doctors help keep
the cows healthy.

The cows must have grass
and other good foods.
Their milk tastes better
when they eat good food.

The milk must be kept cool.
Cool milk does not spoil
as fast as warm milk.

The milk will go by trucks
to a creamery.

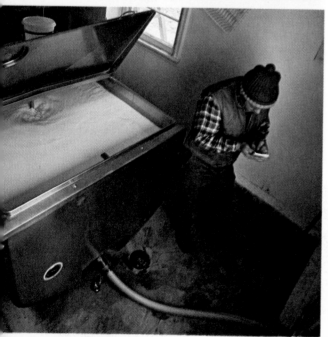

Look at the picture
of the dairy farm.
Now look at the map
of the dairy farm.
What does the map
key show you?

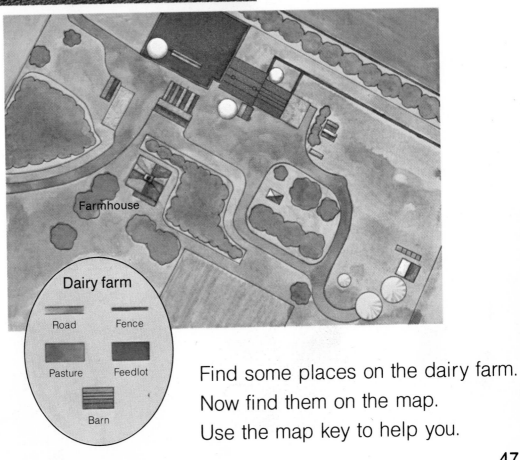

Farmhouse

Dairy farm

Road Fence

Pasture Feedlot

Barn

Find some places on the dairy farm.
Now find them on the map.
Use the map key to help you.

Milk at the creamery

All of the milk is put into a machine.
The machine keeps the milk moving.
The machine keeps the milk cold.

The milk is used in many ways
at the creamery.
A machine puts some of it into cartons.

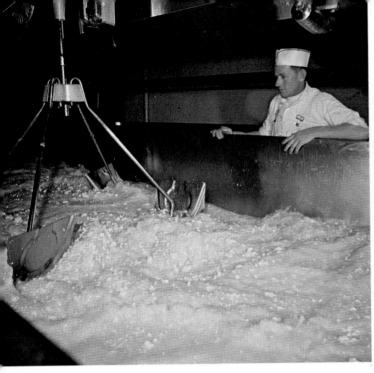

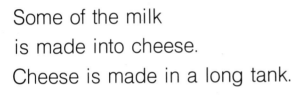

Some of the milk
is made into cheese.
Cheese is made in a long tank.

Some of the cream
from the milk
is made into butter.
Butter is made
in a churn.

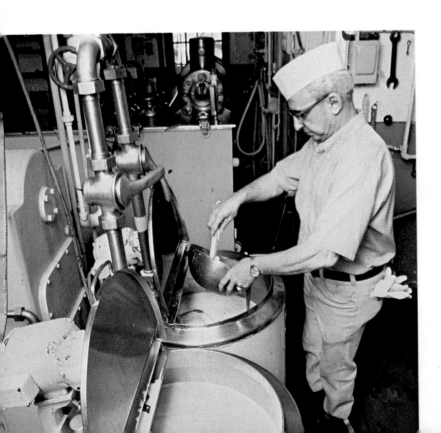

Ice cream is also made
at the creamery.

A vegetable farm

The Garcia farm is like
a giant garden.
In summer they grow vegetables
in the big fields.

In winter it is too cold for plants
to grow in the fields.
Then they grow vegetables
in a greenhouse.
The walls and roof are made
of glass.
Sunlight warms the greenhouse.
Sunlight helps plants grow.

The children went to see the greenhouse.

"We grow tomatoes in the greenhouse
when winter comes," said Mr. Garcia.
"We plant seeds in good soil.
They grow into little green plants.
Then we move each little plant
into a big box.
Later we have large ripe tomatoes.
We sell them to the people nearby."

Tomatoes for you

In summer workers pick the tomatoes.
They are packed in boxes.
Trucks take the tomatoes to a market.

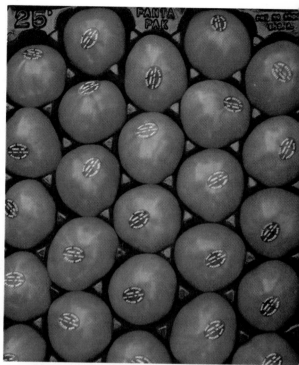

Managers of food stores buy
the tomatoes at the market.
People come to the store to buy
all kinds of food.
They buy the Garcias' tomatoes.

52

Many tomatoes are grown in huge fields.
They are picked by machines.
Trucks haul them to canning factories.
The tomatoes are cooked and put in cans.
They will not spoil in the cans.

The canned tomatoes are sold to stores.
People go to the stores to buy food.
Some will buy canned tomatoes.

A special farm

Scientists work on special farms.
They find better ways to grow plants.
They study fruits and vegetables.

They study the soil.
They find out what will grow
in the soil.
They tell farmers how to make
the soil better.

Scientists also study farm animals.
They help farmers grow healthy
farm animals.
They help farmers grow
bigger animals.

A map helps you

Some foods for Eastfield grow on farms.
Find Eastfield on the map.
Find the farms.

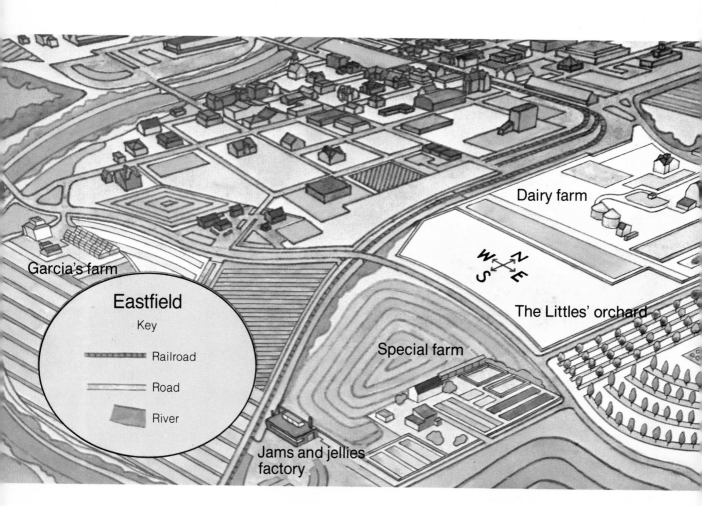

Garcia's farm

Dairy farm

The Littles' orchard

Special farm

Eastfield

Key

━━━━━ Railroad

━━━━━ Road

▬▬▬ River

Jams and jellies
factory

Where is the jams and jellies factory?
Why is it built next to a railroad?
Where is the Garcia farm?
Is it near a good road?
How does the road help the Garcias?

Wheat

Most wheat is grown on large farms.
Those farms are far from Eastfield.
Wheat is used to make many foods.
Which of these foods do you eat?

Farmers get the soil ready.
Then a machine puts wheat seeds in the soil.

Wheat grows from a tiny seed.
At first wheat looks like green grass.
Then it grows tall and changes to golden yellow.
There are many wheat farms in our country.
The map shows where wheat farms are.

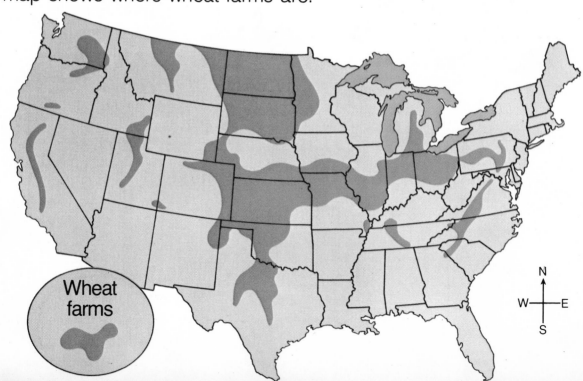

Wheat
farms

N
W— —E
S

A machine cuts the wheat
when it is ripe.
The machine takes the grain
from the top of the plant.

Trucks take some
of the wheat
to a large building.
It is called a grain elevator.

Buckets take grain from the trucks.
The buckets are lifted to the top
of the grain elevator.
The wheat is poured into storage bins.
It is stored until someone buys it.

Much wheat is shipped to flour mills
by truck, train, and ship.
There it is ground into flour.

The bakery

The bakery uses flour to make bread.
A big machine mixes dough.
The dough is put into big pans.

Why are the pans put
in a warm room?

Machines divide the dough into loaves.
The loaves are put into small pans.
The loaves of bread are baked
in a large oven.

What other foods
are made from flour?

Meat

Far away from Eastfield there is
another kind of farm.
It is called a ranch.

Calves are raised on a ranch.
In spring there are many calves.
They eat the grass on the ranch.

Why do families who own ranches
need a great deal of land?

The calves grow big.
Then they need grain to eat.

The calves are sent to farms
far away from the ranch.
The calves have grain to eat
on these farms.
These farms are called feeder farms.

The calves grow bigger.
Then they are ready for market.

Trucks and trains take them to market.

Meat packers buy calves
at the market.

Meat packers get meat ready for stores.
They sell the meat to the stores.
People buy the meat from the stores.

Find the ranch lands on the map.
The map key will help you.

South St. Paul

Milwaukee

Sioux City

Omaha

Kansas City

Oklahoma City

Ft. Worth

N
W — E
S

Ranch lands

Ranch lands   Feeder farm area

Meat packing center

65

The food store

We buy food at stores.
There are many kinds of food.
Food comes to stores
from many places.

There are many workers in a store.
We can see some work that they do.
But we cannot see all of it.

What other work do they do?

We pay money for food.
This money helps pay the workers
who bring us food.

What workers do you see
in the pictures?
What other workers help bring food
to us?

3

We need clothes

The lost jacket

Linda had a busy day.
Where did Linda go?
What did she forget?

Linda could not find her jacket.

Her father said, "No jacket.
No new ice skates.
We do not have money for both
a jacket and ice skates.
I'm sorry, Linda. You must earn
the money for the ice skates."

A new jacket for Linda

Linda and her father went
to a clothing store.
A clerk showed them many jackets.
He showed them jackets made
of different kinds of cloth.

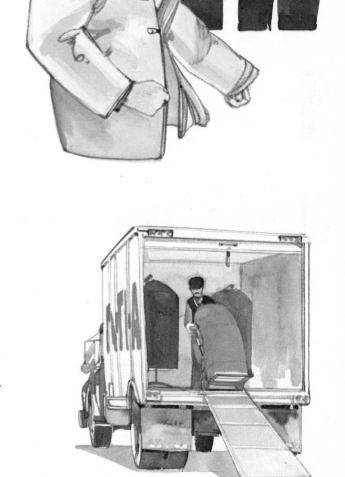

Linda found a jacket she liked.
What did the jacket look like?

Where do you think it came from?
How did it get to the clothing store?
Why do we all need clothes?

Cloth for our clothes

Cloth is made of yarn.
A piece of yarn can be pulled apart.
The yarn is made of thin threads.
These threads are called fibers.

Making fibers into yarn
is called spinning.
Long ago yarn was made
on a spinning wheel.

Machines now
spin fibers into yarn.

Yarn can be made into cloth by weaving.
Long ago weaving was done on a small loom.
Weaving cloth took a long time.
Machines do it much faster today.
Most clothes are made of woven cloth.

Some cloth is made by knitting yarn.
Does anyone in your family know
how to knit?

Today big machines knit yarn into cloth.
Some clothes are made of knitted cloth.

Wool for our cloth

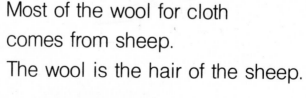

Most of the wool for cloth
comes from sheep.
The wool is the hair of the sheep.

In springtime the wool is cut
from the sheep.
The sheep will grow more wool.

The wool is sent to woolen mills.
There a machine combs and washes it.
Long ago combing was done by hand.
A spinning machine twists
the wool fibers into yarn.
A loom weaves the yarn into cloth.

Use the pictures to help you
tell the story of wool.

Cotton for our cloth

Cotton comes from a plant.
The cotton plant has round,
green bolls growing on it.

The cotton bolls open.
They are then ready to be picked.
The boll is filled with soft,
white cotton fibers.
Seeds are mixed with the cotton fibers.

Sometimes workers pick the cotton.
Sometimes machines pick the cotton.

Machines remove the seeds from the cotton.
Then the cotton fibers are sent
to cotton mills.
Machines at the cotton mill spin
the fibers into yarn.
Other machines weave the yarn into cloth.

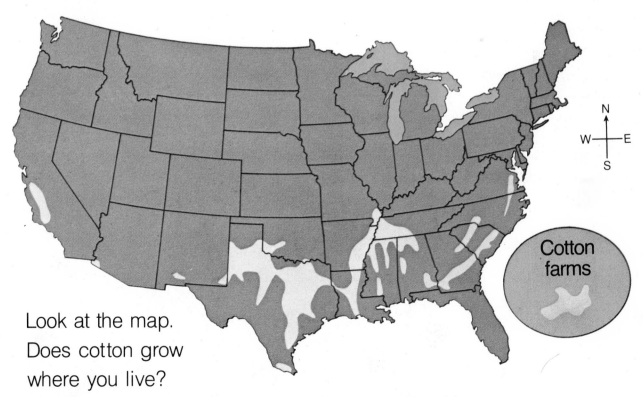

Cotton
farms

Look at the map.
Does cotton grow
where you live?

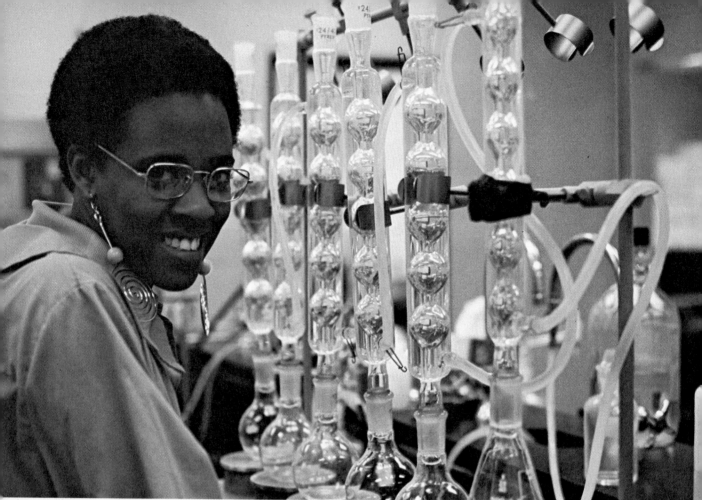

Cloth made by chemists

Many fibers for cloth come
from plants and animals.
There are other kinds
of fibers for cloth.
Some fibers are made from chemicals.

Chemists learned how to make fibers
from chemicals.
The fibers were woven into cloth.
Rayon was the first cloth made
from chemical fibers.

Now there are many kinds of fibers
made from chemicals.
Chemicals are mixed to make a liquid.
This liquid comes out of tiny holes
in a machine.
The streams of liquid harden
into long fibers.

Machines spin the fibers into yarn.
Looms weave the yarn into cloth.

Where clothes are made

All of these people help make clothes.

Designers plan how the clothes will look.

They may use cloth made from chemicals to make clothes.

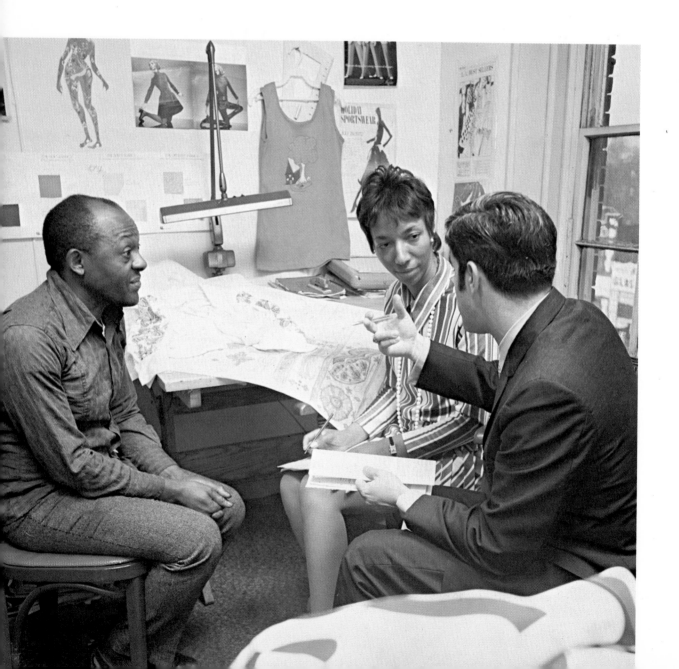

Pattern makers make patterns
for the clothes.
Cutters cut the cloth to match
the patterns.

Workers sew the cloth pieces together
on sewing machines.

Where grandfather works

This is a very special day.
Tony and Rita are having lunch at a store.
Their grandfather works at the store.
It is a big department store.

The store has many departments.
One department sells pots and pans.
Another department sells coats
and dresses.
The sports department sells ice skates,
baseball bats, and boats.

How can you get from floor to floor
in the store?

Many people work in the store

Anna Como is one of the buyers
for the store.
She knows what kinds of clothes
people like.
She buys clothes for the store
from a clothing factory.

A buyer has many helpers.
What kinds of work do they do?

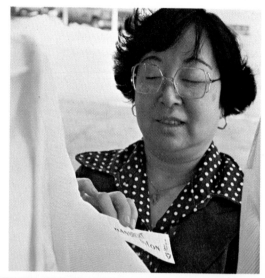

Workers in the office make out bills
for the department store.
Bills are sent to people
who owe money to the store.
Other workers also take in money
for the store.
Grandfather and other workers
get their pay from the office.

Who helps people buy clothes?
Who helps keep the store safe?
Which workers take care of bills?
What work does Rita's grandfather do?

The store uses money

The store pays money for many things.
It must pay its bills.
Bills are sent to the store by clothing factories.
There is a bill for electric light
and a bill for telephones.
In winter there is a bill for fuel.

The store keeps its money at a bank.
The store uses the money that is
in the bank to pay bills.

Saving money

Linda wants to buy ice skates.
What can she do to earn the money?

Linda saves some of her money.
She can buy the ice skates
when she saves enough money.

People save money to buy many things.
Some people save money every week.
Other people save it every month.

How do people save money?
Where do they put the money they save?

4
We need to communicate

People to people

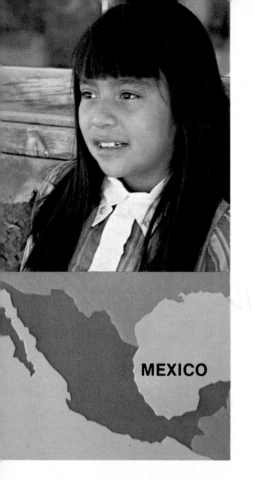

MEXICO

We talk in many languages

Most of us speak English
because we live in the
United States.
Some of us also speak
other languages.

People came to the United States
from many countries.
They brought their languages
with them. Now many people
can speak two languages.

JAPAN

GREECE

The telephone

Tina used the telephone
to call Jim.
She wants him to come to her
birthday party.

What do you think they said?

Bill's mother called the airport.
She must go to New York City.
What do you think
she must find out?

The weather is very cold.
Mr. Kent's furnace is not working.
He needs help.
What kind of worker would he call?

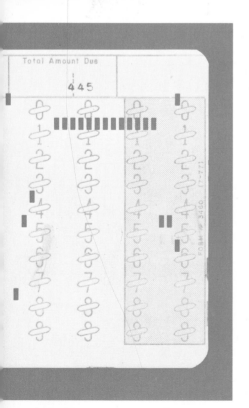

Many workers help you make
a telephone call.
Each worker has a special job.
They must be paid for the jobs they do.
Some workers must have trucks, tools,
and machines. These cost money.

People who use telephones help pay
for all of this.
The telephone company sends them a bill.
The bill tells how much to pay
for one month.
Why may the bill be different each month?

The radio

Police officers and fire fighters
use two-way radios.
So do airplane pilots and
taxi drivers.

Why are they called two-way radios?

Many truck and car drivers use two-way radios.

What do we call the radios they use?
How does the radio help these workers?
What two-way radio can you use?

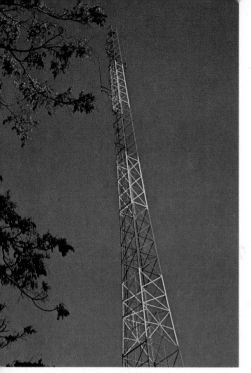

A visit to a radio station

Jean visited the radio station
with her class.
They saw the radio tower.

"My brother has a radio," said Jean.
"He listens to music every evening.
He can even carry his radio with him."

"He has a one-way radio,"
said Miss Wells.
"The music comes from the
radio station.
Each station has its own number.
You tune a radio to that number."

The class went into the studio.
Miss Wells told them about studio signals.
"The red light says, 'The show
is on the air.'"

Miss Wells drew circles
in the air. "This tells the
announcer to talk faster."
She drew a finger across
her throat. "What do you
think this says?"

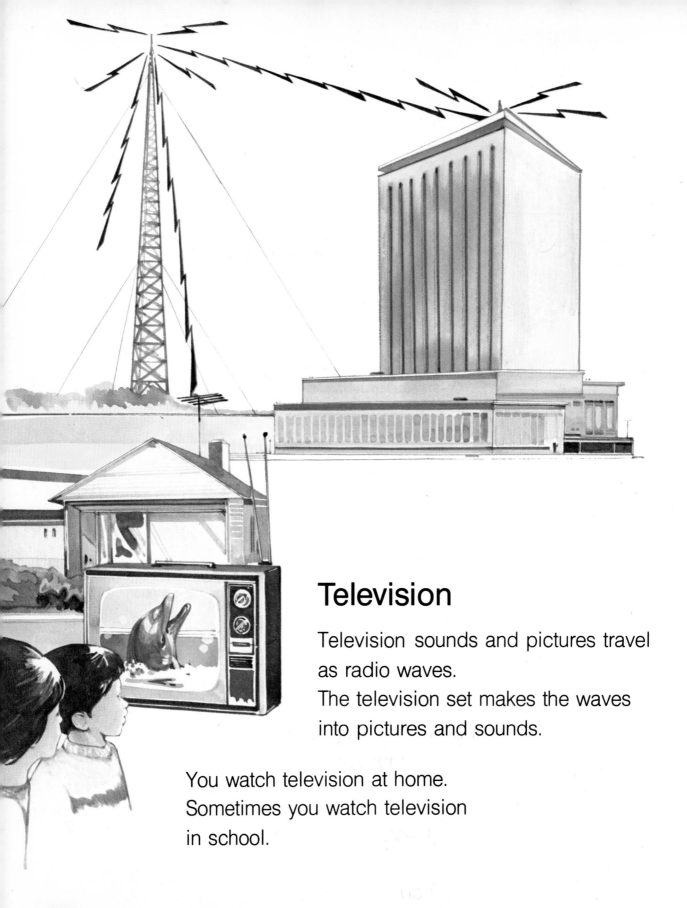

Television

Television sounds and pictures travel
as radio waves.
The television set makes the waves
into pictures and sounds.

You watch television at home.
Sometimes you watch television
in school.

At the television studio

Bob's mother works
at a television studio.
She is taking pictures for a program.
The program is about pets.

A dog food company pays
for the program.
Part of the program tells about dog food.
The company wants people to buy
its dog food.

Bob's dog is a television star.
Her name is Dusty.
She helps sell the dog food.

Some television studios move
around in trucks.
Television workers use special cameras.
They take them where things are happening.
They go to parades and ball games.
They make programs at zoos.

What television programs
do you like best?
Which programs are made
inside a studio?
Which ones are made outside?

What are satellites?

You live on a satellite in space.
It is the earth.
It moves around the sun.
The earth is a satellite
of the sun.

The earth has a satellite.
It is the moon.
The moon moves around the earth.

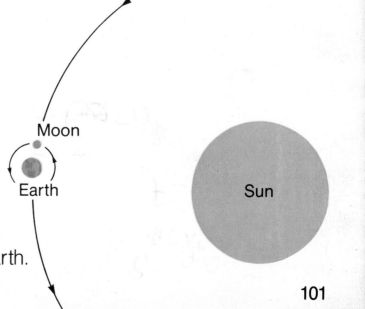

Scientists have made satellites.
They move around the earth.
Scientists put cameras
on these satellites.
The cameras take pictures
of the earth.

How do scientists use
these pictures?

Television programs are sent
to us from across the ocean.
The TV waves are sent
to a satellite.
Then the waves are sent
from the satellite to us.
Satellites help send sounds
and pictures a long way.

What program have you seen that
comes by satellite?

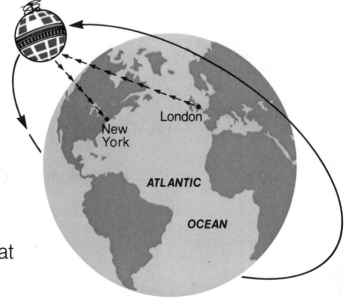

London

New
York

ATLANTIC

OCEAN

A letter for Bob

Bob said, "Here comes Mrs. Ross.
I hope she has some mail for me."

Bob knew he should get a check
for Dusty's work on TV.

"Good morning, Bob," said Mrs. Ross.
"I have some mail for you."

"Good," said Bob. "Thank you."

Bob and his mother went to the bank.
Bob wrote his name on the back
of the check.

He was given money for the check.
"Thank you, Dusty," said Bob.

Bob's check came by mail.
It had been put into a mail box
near the television studio.

A post-office worker came
to the box in a truck.
The worker picked up all
of the mail from the box.
The truck took the mail
to the post office.

Workers at the post office
helped unload the mail
from the truck.

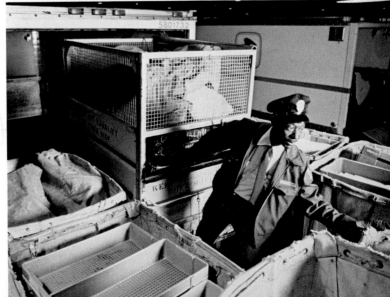

The post office

Machines mark each stamp
with black lines.
This mark tells that the stamp
has been used.

The machines also print the date
the letter was mailed.
They also print the name of the town.

Other machines sort the letters
by zip codes.
A zip code is a number that tells
where a letter is to go.
Letters without zip codes take longer
to sort.
What is your zip code?

People pay money for stamps.
Stamps help pay post-office workers.
The money pays for machines
and post-office buildings, too.

Much mail is carried by airplanes.
How do letters get to the airport?

Some mail is carried by trucks.
Little trucks pick up mail
from mail boxes.
Big trucks move the mail
along the highways.
They also take mail to the airport.

The Eastfield News

"The children in my class
know about Dusty," said Bob.
"They saw Dusty on television.
Now I can show them pictures
of her from the newspaper."

This is the newspaper office
in Eastfield.
Reporters get the news.
They find out what is going on.

Then they write news stories
for the paper.
Some reporters work in Eastfield.
Others work in places far away.

News from nearby comes by telephone.
News from far away comes
by special machines.

Other workers get stories
and pictures ready for the press.

A big press prints the
newspaper. Some pictures
are printed in color.
Trucks rush the newspapers
to places in all parts
of Eastfield. The people
of Eastfield buy papers.

110

The newspaper has ads in it.
Companies pay the newspaper
to print their ads.
How do newspapers use this money?

Look for different kinds
of ads in your newspaper.

Find the comics in your newspaper.
What else can you find
in your newspaper?

Producers

Linda needed money to buy ice skates.
She did different kinds of work
to earn the money.
The work she did is called services.
Linda was a producer of services.

Farmers produce food.
Some workers produce machines.
These producers grow or make things.

Workers in stores produce services.
What other workers produce services?
Workers in factories produce things.
What other workers produce things?

Consumers

Linda bought ice skates.
Linda was a consumer when she bought them.
A consumer buys goods.
Consumers buy food and clothing.
They buy TV sets and radios.

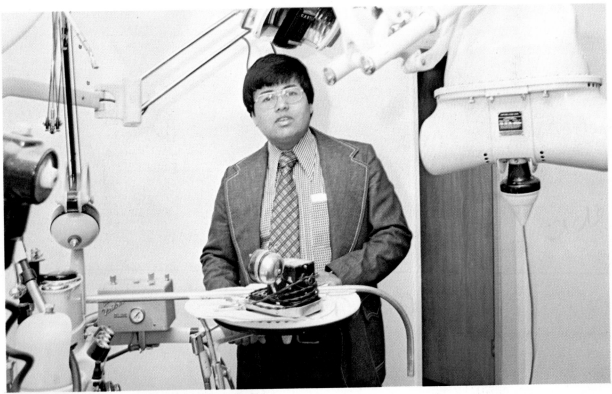

Consumers also buy services.
Consumers pay doctors and dentists for services.
Taxicab and telephone companies sell services to consumers, too.

Producers and consumers

Workers are both producers and consumers.
When they work, they are producers.
When they buy, they are consumers.

In which picture is Janet a consumer?
In which picture is she a producer?

Who in your family are producers?
What do they produce?
When are you a consumer?

5
We travel in many ways

We live in a large country

To what places on the map have you traveled?
Did you travel by car?
In what other ways did you travel?

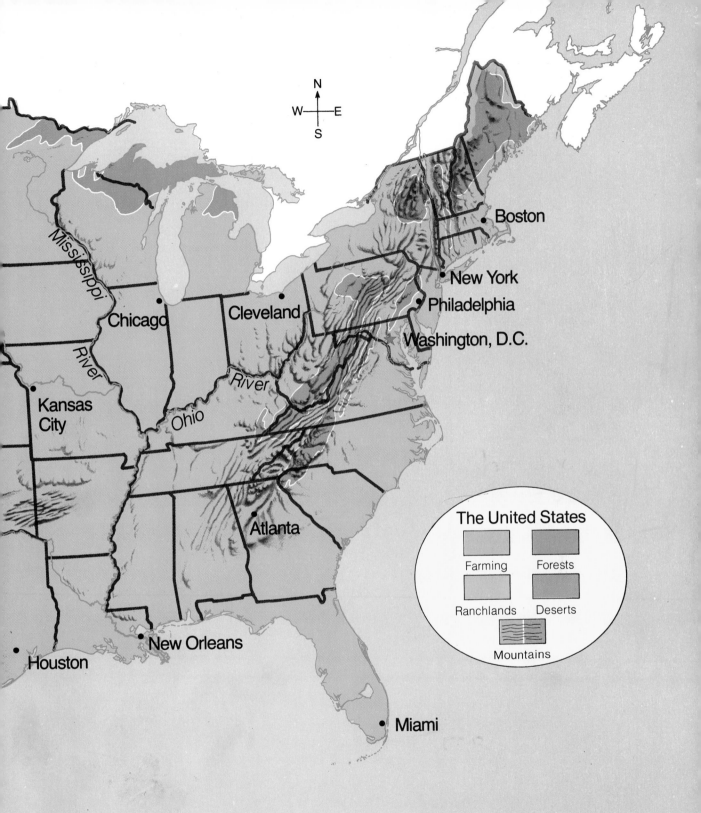

N
W · E
S

Boston

New York
Philadelphia
Washington, D.C.

Mississippi

River

River

Ohio

Chicago

Cleveland

Kansas
City

Atlanta

New Orleans

Houston

Miami

The United States

Farming   Forests

Ranchlands   Deserts

Mountains

117

Traveling by jet

Alicia Ortega works for a company.
The company makes cars.
Her work takes her far from home.
She travels by jet to save time.
Sometimes she takes a taxi to the airport.

Look at the pictures.
What did Alicia Ortega do
with her suitcase?

What is the worker loading on the jet?

In which picture is the jet
getting fuel for the flight?

Other workers are looking carefully
at the jet.
They are making sure it is safe
for its flight.

The workers in the tower
are talking to the pilots
in the jet.
What are they
talking about?

These pilots fly the jet.
They watch many dials.
The dials tell how the plane
is running.

The pilots are very busy when
they are on a flight.
They must fly the plane safely.

Alicia Ortega is busy, too.
She is planning ways
to sell new cars.

What other workers
do you see?
What are they doing?

Alicia Ortega paid to ride on the jet.
She paid the airline that owns the jet.

The airline uses this money in many ways.
The money is used to pay workers.
It is used to buy fuel.
The airline uses money to buy new jets.
It must pay to use the airport.

Traveling in the city

Many people live and work in a city.
How do they get to work?
How do they go shopping?
How do they travel to other places?

Tony and his family live
in Washington, D.C.
They use different ways to travel
in Washington.

Often the streets are crowded
with buses, cars, and trucks.
Cars move very slowly then.
When cars move very slowly,
they use much gasoline.

Most of the time Tony's family travels on the new subway.

A subway is a train that travels under the ground.

How does it make the streets less crowded?

How does the subway save gasoline?

Traveling by train

Marie lives in Chicago.
She is going to visit in Flagstaff.
She will travel part way by train.

She went to the train station by bus.
Her train was ready to leave on time.

Find Chicago and Flagstaff
on the map on pages 116 and 117.
Look at the map key.

How are mountains shown?

The railroad has many workers.
Some work to make
train travel safe.
Some help to run the train.
Others take care of the people
who travel on the train.

In the mountains

The locomotive pulled the train
through many kinds of land.
First came the plains.
Then came the Rocky Mountains.

Marie saw tall mountain peaks.
They were covered with snow.
Some snow stays
on the tallest peaks all year.

Marie saw streams and waterfalls.
The water came from the snow.

Marie saw lakes and forests.
She saw lovely meadows, too.
The meadow grass was very green.

There is plenty of water
high up in the mountains.
Much rain falls in spring and in summer.
In the winter much snow falls.

There is enough water for tall trees to grow.
There is enough water for grass to grow.

There is plenty of food
for animals in the mountains.
There are grass and leaves.
There are many kinds of plants
to eat.
There are berries and nuts.

Many birds live in the mountains
in summer.
Why do you think that this is so?

In the desert

Then the train traveled across desert lands.

Find the desert lands on the map
on pages 116 and 117. Use the map key.

The desert was very different
from the mountains.
Marie saw plants that were not
like those in the mountains.

Very little rain falls on the desert.
Rain may come only a few times a year.
Plants that grow in the desert
need little water.

Cactus plants are one kind of desert plant.
Cactus plant roots grow near
the top of the ground.
They take in water quickly when it rains.
Water is stored in these plants.

Animals live in the desert, too.
They have ways to live with little water.
Some get water from the plants.
In the daytime animals hide from the hot sun.

Living things of the desert depend
upon the desert.
They also depend upon each other.

Most desert insects live on the plants.
Desert birds live on plants and insects.
Other small animals live on plants and insects.
Large animals and birds may live
on the small animals.

What would happen if desert plants were destroyed?
What would happen if desert insects were destroyed?
What would happen if small animals were destroyed?

Traveling by ship

Jim Wasser lives in Los Angeles.
He is going to Alaska.
He will travel by ship.

Find Los Angeles on the map.
Find Alaska on the map.
The map shows where the ship went.

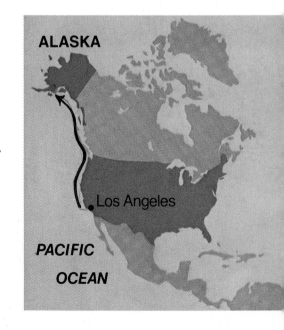

Jim will see the ocean from the ship.
He will see mountains and forests.

Jim's ship left from the harbor
of Los Angeles.
It will sail into a harbor in Alaska.
Harbors are safe places for ships to stay.

How do goods travel?

Some goods travel by ship.
Large ships that carry goods
are called freighters.
Ships carry goods on the ocean
and on lakes and rivers.
They carry all kinds of goods.

Railroads carry goods, too.
Goods are sent all over the country
by train.
Freight trains carry all kinds
of goods in freight cars.

Many goods travel by truck.
Some towns are not near railroads
or rivers or oceans.
Trucks bring goods to the people
of these towns.
Some trucks carry goods all the way
across our country.

Goods that have to travel fast
are shipped by plane.
Food that has to be kept fresh
often travels by plane.

A new home

David and Esther are visiting their grandparents.
The grandparents have a new home in the south.
They live there in the winter.

Grandfather and Grandmother
showed the children their camper.

Grandmother said, "We will stay
in the south this winter.
In the spring we will drive in our camper
across the country."

"We will stay in campgrounds
on our trip," said Grandfather.

"Travel has changed," Grandmother said.
"When my mother was young,
she went to town in a buggy.
It was pulled by a horse."

"Yes," said Grandfather.
"It took three hours to drive to town.
We would now make the trip by car.
The trip would take thirty minutes."

"Things will change even more,"
Grandmother said.
"Someday you may take a rocket
and travel to another planet."

6
Getting to know Japan

Visiting the grandparents

Sumi Okada lives in Tokyo.
She and her mother are visiting
Sumi's grandparents.
They live in a small town near a large park.
Mount Fuji is in this large park.

Sumi had never been so close
to Mount Fuji before.
"Please, Grandfather," Sumi said.
"I want to climb Mount Fuji."

"Not this visit," Grandfather said.
"We will wait until we have more time."

Sumi's grandparents are farmers.
They raise rice, which grows in water.
Growing rice is hard work.
But they have a machine
to help them.

Sumi's grandparents like
the Japanese clothes of long ago.
So Sumi wears her kimono when she visits them.

In a few days Sumi and her mother said good-by.
They left for home in Tokyo.

139

Sumi was sad to leave her
grandmother and grandfather.
But she smiled when she thought
about her next visit.
Grandfather had said that they
would climb Mount Fuji.

Soon Sumi and Mrs. Okada reached Tokyo.
Tokyo is the largest city in the world.
There are many autos, trucks,
and buses on the streets.

What problems do they cause the city?

Going to work

The Okadas live in a small house
on the edge of Tokyo.
Mr. Okada goes to work each day
on a fast electric train.
The train is crowded when people
are going to work.
It is crowded when people
are coming home from work.

Mrs. Okada works, too.
She works in a shop
where motorcycles are sold.
Mrs. Okada takes Sumi to school
on her way to work.

Sumi comes home from school
with her friend Tara.
Tara lives in an apartment house.
She lives near Sumi.

At home

In Japan people do not wear shoes in the house.
The Okadas take off their shoes outside.
Then they put on slippers.

The family has tea as soon as
everyone is home.
Sometimes they ask friends
to have tea with them.
Tea time is a quiet time.

143

Mother and Sumi go shopping

Mrs. Okada and Sumi visited
a department store in Tokyo.
There are many stores and shops
in downtown Tokyo.

They looked at the new fall clothes.
First Mother bought Sumi a raincoat.
Then she bought her a kimono.

Tara is Sumi's best friend.
Sumi bought a present for Tara.
It was a baseball.
Sumi and Tara like to play baseball.

Parks in the city

Tokyo has many buildings.
The buildings are close together.
There are many people on the streets.
"Let's visit Meiji Park,"
said Mother.

There were trees and flowers in Meiji Park.
It was a quiet place to stop
and rest in the busy city.

"Today is Saturday," Mother said.
"Father works until noon.
We will meet him in Ueno Park
and have lunch there."

Mrs. Okada and Sumi took a subway
to Ueno Park.
Many people were traveling on the subway.
The subway would be very crowded later.
Then many workers and shoppers
would be going home.

Sumi, Father, and Mother ate lunch.
The Okadas eat mostly fish,
vegetables, and rice.

Japan has little land for cattle.
Japan has water around it.
Fish is easy to get at low prices.

After lunch they explored the park.

Look at the pictures on this page.
What are some things they saw?

A visit to Japan

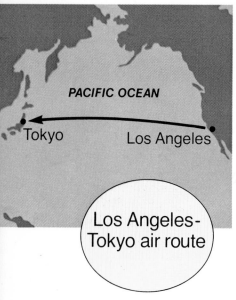

PACIFIC OCEAN

Tokyo   Los Angeles

Los Angeles-
Tokyo air route

The Yoshidas are visiting Japan.
They took a jet from Los Angeles to Tokyo.
Then they took the monorail into Tokyo.
Their children, Sharon and David,
are with them.

The Yoshidas saved money for the trip.
They saved for a long time.
It costs a great deal of money
to travel to Japan.

Mr. and Mrs. Yoshida want Sharon
and David to see many places.

There are many ways to travel
in Japan.
In the city the family used subways
and buses.

Japan has good highways
for traveling around the country.
Some people travel by airplane.

Mr. Yoshida said, "Tomorrow
we will go to Kyoto.
We will ride on the fastest
train in the world."

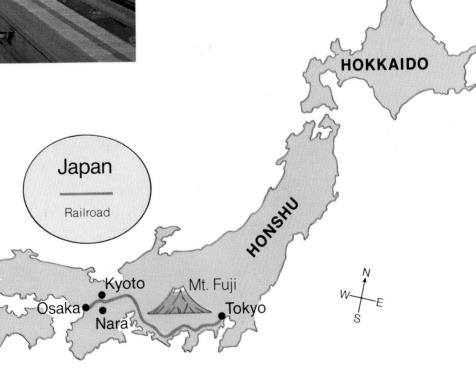

Japan

Railroad

HOKKAIDO

HONSHU

KYUSHU

Kyoto
Osaka
Nara
Mt. Fuji
Tokyo

N
W E
S

Their Aunt Mitsuo and Uncle Noboru
live in the city of Kyoto.
For a thousand years Kyoto was
the capital of Japan.

Sharon and David saw many
things in Kyoto.
They visited beautiful old buildings
and gardens.

Mrs. Yoshida said, "The Japanese love
the outdoor world.
They feel that things in the outdoor world
are beautiful."

Sharon and David met
many people from all parts
of Japan in Kyoto.
People like to come to Kyoto
in the spring.
Many flowers are in bloom
in spring.

Kyoto is a very old city.
People come to see the buildings.
The buildings help them think
about the past.

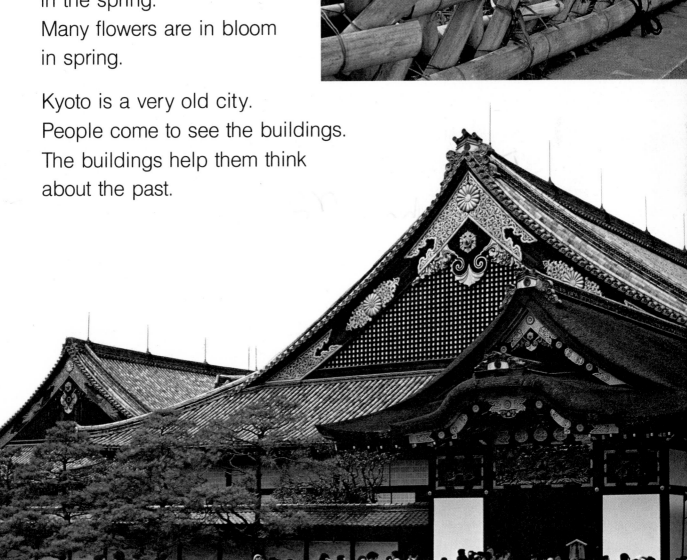

Mr. Yoshida said, "Today we will go
to Osaka.
Osaka is a very large city.
All kinds of goods are made
in factories in Osaka."
The Yoshidas visited a factory
where machinery is made.

They saw the busy harbor of Osaka.
Many freighters were in the harbor.
The freighters carry away goods made in Osaka.
Some bring food for the people of Osaka.

"Let's go to Nara!" the children said.
"Let's go to Deer Park."

The Yoshidas stayed at an inn in Nara.
They all wore slippers inside the inn.

Sharon and David fed the deer
at Deer Park.
They bought rice cookies to feed the deer.

"Be careful," Mother said.
"Don't turn your back on a hungry deer.
He may give you a push to tell you
he's hungry."

We trade with Japan

"Mother," Sharon said, "why does Japan get food from other places?"

"Only a little land can be used for farms," Mother answered. "There are so many mountains.

"Rice is grown on some of the land on the mountain sides. But not enough food can be grown to feed all of the people.

"Japan is a group of islands. So much of its food is from the ocean."

Mr. Yoshida said, "Food must
be bought from other countries.
The company where I work
sells food to Japan."

Japan has very little oil and coal.
Oil and coal are needed for the factories.
Gasoline is needed for cars and trucks.

How do you think the Japanese
pay for all of the things they buy?

There are many thousands of factories
in Japan.
They make all kinds of goods.
Japan sells many of these goods
in the United States.
It sells goods to other countries, too.

Look at the pictures on these pages.
What are some of the things
that Japan sells?

It was time for the Yoshidas
to go home.
Sharon and David
enjoyed their visit.
They enjoyed seeing relatives.
They enjoyed learning
about Japan.
But they were happy
to be going home.

Dictionary

city

farm

island

bakery A place where bread, cakes, and similar foods are made

city A place where many people live and work

cotton A fluffy white material that grows on a plant and is used for cloth

desert Land where very little rain falls

factory A place where things are made

farm Land on which plants or animals are raised

forest Land covered with many trees

harbor A safe place for ships to load and unload

hill Raised land, not as high as a mountain

island A piece of land that has water all around it

jacket A short coat

jet A strong stream of gas or liquid
An airplane moved by such a stream is called a jet.

lake A body of water that has land all around it

mountain

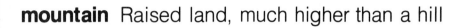

mountain Raised land, much higher than a hill

ocean A very large body of salt water. The sea

orchard Land covered with fruit trees

post office A place where mail is handled

river A large stream of fresh water

ship A large boat

ship

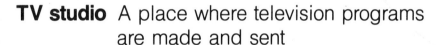

TV studio A place where television programs are made and sent

telephone An object used to send voices or sound by electricity

train A line of railroad cars pulled by an engine

wheat A grass-like plant that produces a grain we grind into flour and use in bread and other foods

train

wool The hair or fur that grows on sheep and is used for cloth

Credits

Graphic Design and Production
Edit, Inc.

Maps
Leon Bishop: 15, 19, 28-29, 47, 58, 65, 77, 149
Edit, Inc.: 92, 132, 148
Robert C. Forget: 116-117

Illustrations
Leon Bishop: 9, 11, 13, 25, 30, 56
Edit, Inc.: 101, 103
Chuck Mitchell: 135, 136
Charles Robinson: 138, 139, 140, 141, 142, 143, 144, 146
Dan Siculan: 16, 18, 64, 111
Joel Snyder: 34, 36, 38, 51, 70, 71, 88, 90, 91, 96, 97, 98, 99, 104, 108, 112, 113, 114
John Walter & Associates:
Ray App, 120
Suzanne Snider, 123

Photographs
J. C. Allen and Son: 51, 58
American Textile Manufacturers Institute: 78 top
Peter Arnold:
Bruce Curtis, 100 center
W. H. Hodge, 140
Jacques Jangoux, 156 right
Yoram Kahane, 144 bottom
Krasenaur, 159 bottom
Harvey Lloyd, 152 bottom, 155 bottom
Werner Rau, 154-155 top
James L. Ballard: 3 left, 4, 69, 82, 83 top left and top right, 84, 86, 87, 92 bottom left and bottom right, 115, 120 bottom, 121, 153 bottom, 157, 158 top and bottom
Black Star:
Dennis Brack, 108-109
Fred Ward, 158 center
Brownberry Ovens, Division of Peavy Co.: 61 bottom left
Burlington Northern: 60 top, 125 bottom, 133 bottom
Butterick Fashion Marketing Co.: 81 top right
California Canners and Growers: 53 top
Carnation: 53 bottom left and bottom right

Colonial Williamsburg Foundation: 17 top
Consulate General of Japan, N.Y.: 32 right
Cooperstown Indian Museum: 15
DPI:
J. Alex Langley, 141 right, 143, 144 top, 150 top
DuPont: 78 bottom
Ex-Cello Corp.: 48
Food Marketing Institute: 66 top
Genesco, Inc.: 81 top left
Harlow Old Fort House, Plymouth, Mass.: 72 left, 73 left, 75 bottom
Grant Heilman: 31 top, 35, 44, 45, 46 top, 50 top, 54-55, 57, 59 right
Edwin Hoffman, 134 bottom right
Illinois Bell Telephone Co.: 94 top left
The Image Bank:
Bullaty Lomeo, 32 top
Wolf van dem Bussche, 119 left
Japan National Tourist Organization: 147 top
Jereboam:
Ron Lickers, 113 center
Vincent J. Kamin & Associates:
Dan Morrill, 128 bottom right
Steven C. Wilson, 128 top
Magnum:
Erich Hartmann, 125 top
Marilyn Silverstone, 153 top left
Herb & Dorothy McLaughlin: 62, 74 top, 131 top left
Meyers Photo Art:
Jaeggi, 112 bottom
Monkmeyer: 92 top
Dan Morrill: 26 right, 126 top, 127, 129 top, 130 top, 159 center
David Muench: 12 right, 126 bottom
National Aeronautics & Space Administration: 101, 102, 103, 136
Photo Researchers:
Roger A. Clark, Jr., 94 top right, 110 top right
Jack Fields, 137
Robert A. Isaacs, 139 left
Albert Knaus, 150 bottom
Paolo Koch, 152 top

Tom McHugh, 27 right
National Audubon Society Collection:
R. Grogan, 133 top
Rapho Division:
Brian Brake, 154 bottom left
Dana Levy, 151 top
H. W. Silvester, 154 bottom right
Lawrence L. Smith, 151 bottom
Photri:
Taurus Photos, 11 bottom, 31 bottom
Reflejo/Vincent J. Kamin & Associates: 20 bottom, 65 top, 67 top and right, 106 center right, 107 top, 134 bottom left
G. R. Roberts: 30 bottom, 67 bottom, 77 top
B. Rogers: 146 bottom, 153 top right
Root Resources:
Anthony Mercieca, 128 bottom left, 130 bottom, 131 top right and bottom right
Santa Fe Railway: 124 top
Scott-d'Arazien: 72 bottom right, 73 top and bottom, 75 top, 79 bottom
Sekai Bunka Photo: 141 left, 145 bottom, 148, 156 left, 159 top
Shostal Associates: 110 middle left
Art d'Arazien, 77 right
E. S. Bernard, 95 bottom, 99
Eric Carle, 46 center, 65 right, 66 bottom, 118
Dwight Elleffsen, 119 bottom right
David Forbert, 79 top, 80
Tony Linck, 90
David Muench, 135
Dick Patterson, 120 top
Alvin Upitis, 61 top and bottom right, 81 bottom right
Bert Vogel, 133 center
Howard Simmons Photography Inc.: 1, 2, 3 right, 5, 6, 7, 8, 9, 10, 12 left, 14, 17 right and bottom, 20 top, 21, 22, 23, 24, 25, 33, 49 bottom, 68, 72 top right, 83 bottom, 85, 89, 93, 96, 97, 105, 106 top left and bottom left, 109 top right and bottom, 110 bottom

The J. M. Smucker Co.: 39 top, 40 top, 41 bottom, 42, 43
Bob & Ira Spring: 149 bottom
Tom Stack & Associates:
Paul Meyer, 129 bottom
Dave Scheffer, 145 top
Bob Wick, 138
Stock, Boston:
Daniel Brody, 13 top
P. Chock, 32 bottom
W. B. Finch, 26 left
Gwen Franken, 113 bottom
Owen Franken, 26 bottom, 27 left, 113 bottom
Ellis Herwig, 119 top right
Levi Strauss Co.: 81 bottom left
Taurus Photos:
Dr. E. R. Degginger, 132 top
L. L. T. Rhodes, 13 bottom, 95 top, 134 top
Wm. R. Wright, 124 bottom
U.S. Department of Agriculture: 112 center
U.S. Postal Service: 106 center left, 107 center and bottom
Washington Apple Commission: 37 top
WBBM-TV, Chicago: 100 top and bottom
Webb•Ag Photos: 37 bottom, 38, 40 bottom, 41 top, 46 bottom left and bottom right, 47, 49 left and right, 50 bottom, 52, 54, 55, 59 left, 60 bottom, 63 top, 64, 74, center and bottom, 76, 118
Welch's Company: 39 bottom
Woodfin Camp & Associates:
Marc & Evelyne Bernheim, 11 top left
Jeffrey Foxx, 11 top right
George Hall, 27 center
Thomas Horker, 147 bottom
Marvin E. Newman, 63 bottom
Leo de Wys, Inc.:
Peter Dublin, 139 right
Everett C. Johnson, 122 top and bottom, 123
Rick Smolan, 149 top

EFGH083210
Printed in the United States of America